Captain Kidd

by Sue Hamilton

Visit us at
www.abdopublishing.com

Published by ABDO Publishing Company, 4940 Viking Drive, Suite 622, Edina, Minnesota 55435.
Copyright ©2007 by Abdo Consulting Group, Inc. International copyrights reserved in all countries.
No part of this book may be reproduced in any form without written permission from the publisher.
ABDO & Daughters™ is a trademark and logo of ABDO Publishing Company.

Printed in the United States.

Editors: John Hamilton/Tad Bornhoft
Graphic Design: John Hamilton/Sue Hamilton
Cover Design: Neil Klinepier
Cover Illustration: *Captain Kidd*, ©1996 Don Maitz; *Pegleg*, ©1996 Don Maitz
Interior Photos and Illustrations: p 1 *Captain Kidd*, ©1996 Don Maitz; p 3 *Dead Men Tell No Tales*,
©2003 Don Maitz; p 5 *Relaxing on Deck* by Howard Pyle, Mary Evans; p 7 Kidd in battle, Getty;
p 9 Kidd on deck with ladies, Getty; p 11 King William III, North Wind; p 12 Jeremy Roch's *Charles
Galley*, courtesy National Maritime Museum, Greenwich, England; p 13 *Eyes for Prize*, ©2005
Don Maitz; p 14-15 Men pressed into service, North Wind; p 16 Map of Kidd's range, Cartesia/
Hamilton; p 17 *Burying Treasure* by Howard Pyle, Mary Evans; p 18-19 *Captain Kidd* ©1996 Don
Maitz; p 21 Kidd hitting gunner with bucket, Corbis; p 22 Map, Mariners' Museum; p 23 Mogul
of India, Mary Evans; p 25 Governor Coote, courtesy the Library of Harvard University; p 27 (top)
Kidd accused of piracy, North Wind; (bottom) Kidd's note to the king, Corbis; p 29 Kidd hanging,
North Wind; p 31 Digging for Kidd's treasure, North Wind

Library of Congress Cataloging-in-Publication Data

Hamilton, Sue L., 1959-
  Captain Kidd / Sue Hamilton.
     p. cm. -- (Pirates)
  Includes index.
  ISBN-13: 978-1-59928-759-1
  ISBN-10: 1-59928-759-5
  1. Kidd, William, d. 1701--Juvenile literature. 2. Pirates--Great Britain--Biography--Juvenile
literature. I. Title.

  G537.K5H35 2007
  910.4'5--dc22
  [B]
                                        2006032017

Contents

DEAD MEN TELL NO TALES

William Kidd

The name of Captain William Kidd brings to mind adventure and buried treasure. He was a stern British captain with a violent temper who fought for his king as a privateer. He led a notorious yet unfortunate life. Kidd's shocking trial and execution, and the grisly decay of his body, have never been forgotten. Some claim his treasure is still out there, somewhere, just waiting to be found. Kidd's infamous life ended just after the turn of the 18th century, but not before he made his mark in the Golden Age of Piracy.

Not much is known of Captain Kidd's early life. He may have been born on January 22, 1654, in Dundee, Scotland, although some sources place his birth in Greenock, Scotland, around 1645. Kidd's father might have been a Presbyterian minister. It's also possible the pirate's father was a seaman, since Kidd once listed himself as "born to the sea."

It is a mystery how William Kidd spent his youth. No specifics are known. He probably spent several years at sea, possibly as a deckhand, gaining experience and knowledge on board different ships.

Life in the mid-17th century was not easy. Disease and death were common. The Great Plague of London in 1665-1666 killed a fifth of the city's population, between 75,000 and 100,000 people. It would not be surprising if Kidd followed the example of many others and left Europe aboard a ship to the Americas.

Kidd survived grim odds and grew into a powerful man with a good knowledge of seamanship. However, his attitude was less attractive. He was a heavy drinker, and could often be found in the midst of an argument or fight. He commanded ships by using fear and threats, instead of proving himself through knowledge and courage. He served aboard ships for many long years before a chance opportunity changed his fate.

Facing Page: Relaxing on Deck by Howard Pyle, an illustration of Captain William Kidd.

Blessed William

A privateer was a ship, or its crew, that used a license to attack and capture enemy ships. The license was called a letter of marque. In 1689, Kidd found himself aboard a privateer sailing in the waters of the Caribbean. Kidd was in his mid-30s by now, and an experienced seaman. His ship had a mixed crew of English and French sailors. It was an explosive situation, since the two countries were at war with one another.

Close quarters and political differences caused friction between the French and English crew members. After a bloody fight, the English crew members took control of the ship. The 20-gun vessel sailed to a port on the Caribbean island of Nevis, where it was renamed the *Blessed William*, after England's King William III. Kidd was named captain of the *Blessed William*, and given his own privateering license. He and his crew were paid with whatever booty they took from enemy ships and settlements.

Kidd and his ship later joined forces with ships of the British Royal Navy, attacking French warships and settlements on the island of Marie-Galante. Captain Thomas Hewetson, who headed the Royal Navy's attack, wrote that Kidd "was a mighty man who fought as well as any man I ever saw."

As captain of the ship, Kidd received large rewards. However, his crew was not well paid. Also, Kidd had been ordered to attack French military ships. The crew felt there was little reward and much danger involved in this. Before long, mutiny was in the air.

Led by future pirate Robert Culliford, the crew simply waited until the captain spent a night ashore. Kidd awakened to find himself on Nevis minus a ship, and deprived of all his money and possessions.

Governor Christopher Codrington, thankful for all that Kidd had done to protect the people of Nevis from the French, awarded Kidd a captured French warship, which was renamed the *Antigua*. Kidd set sail for New York, intent on finding the *Blessed William* and arresting the thieves.

There is no proof that Kidd ever found the ship, although undoubtedly he greatly wanted to bring the mutineers to justice. But even though Kidd couldn't find his stolen fortune, he did manage to find a home... and a scandal.

Above: Captain Kidd fights bravely.

New York Revolt

William Kidd sailed to New York in 1690. The colony was in rebellion. The acting governor, Jacob Leisler, refused to step down when Henry Sloughter, newly-appointed by King William III, arrived to take the post as governor in March 1691.

Captain Kidd found himself in a position to help end the revolt. He used his ship to transport weapons and ammunition for Sloughter, assisting the king's representative to end Leisler's rebellion. When the thankful Sloughter finally took his place as governor, he rewarded Kidd with money and a commendation.

Now in his late 30s, tall, well-dressed, and confident, William Kidd quickly became a part of New York society. He met Mrs. Sarah Bradley Cox Oort, the wife of wealthy businessman John Oort. Sarah, a lovely socialite, became friends with William. A few months later, on May 5, 1691, John Oort mysteriously died.

On May 16, 1691, only a few days after Oort's death, Sarah and William Kidd were married. Whether or not the couple had something to do with John's death is unknown. However, rumors spread quickly, especially since this was Sarah's third marriage, and she was only in her 20s.

Sarah's previous two husbands had left her a wealthy widow. She and Kidd owned beautiful homes, including one on Pearl Street on Manhattan Island, near the docks of the old harbor.

In the next few years, Kidd did not stray far from his life on land, although he did keep his ship. He and Sarah had two daughters, Elizabeth and Sarah. The captain helped fund the building of Trinity Church, the oldest church in Manhattan.

Above: Captain William Kidd entertains guests on the deck of his ship. He eventually fell in love with Mrs. Sarah Bradley Cox Oort. Only days after her husband died in 1691, William and Sarah were married.

Sarah's position enabled her husband to meet many of the city's top citizens and political leaders. When Kidd went down to the harbor, he delighted in bragging about his high-ranking friends to any captain or dockworker who would listen.

William Kidd seemed to lead the life of a model citizen. But after four years, the sea captain became bored. He needed adventure, and he would soon find it across the sea, in England.

Adventure Galley

In 1695, Captain William Kidd sailed the *Antigua* from his home and family in New York to England. It was Kidd's intention to secure a captaincy in the Royal Navy. England and France were at war, and he wanted a trained crew to take on the French. However, Kidd found that securing this type of position was nearly impossible.

Instead, Kidd was strongly advised—under threat that his ship, the *Antigua,* would be impounded by His Majesty's Customs—to accept a privateer's commission. This would allow him to "legally" hunt down French vessels and take the spoils to share between himself, his crew, and whoever backed the expedition. With the help of an influential friend from Albany, New York, this plan would soon become a reality.

Fellow Scotsman and friend Robert Livingstone was in England at the same time as Kidd. Livingstone introduced Kidd to Richard Coote, Earl of Bellomont. As the newly appointed Royal Governor of Massachusetts, New Hampshire, and New York, Governor Coote wanted to stop the piracy and smuggling that was occurring regularly in the Americas.

To accomplish his task, Kidd needed a strong, swift ship, and that required money. Governor Coote found financial backing from four of the most influential

Below: Captain William Kidd's original privateering license.

people in England: Charles Talbot, Duke of Shrewsbury and Secretary of State; Henry Sidney, Earl of Romney and Master General of the King's Ordinance; Sir John Somers, Lord Justice; and Admiral Sir Edward Russell, First Lord of the Admiralty and Treasurer of the Navy.

By December 10, 1695, Kidd was granted a privateer's letter of marque. The following month, on January 26, 1696, King William himself granted Kidd a

Above: King William III granted William Kidd a letter of marque.

commission to hunt pirates. However, the king was very specific about what Kidd could and could *not* do:

We do hereby jointly charge and command you, as you will answer the same at your utmost Peril, That you do not, in any manner, offend or molest any of our Friends or Allies, their Ships or Subjects.

With his privateer's commission secure, Kidd searched for a fast ship. He soon found the *Adventure Galley,* a 124-foot (38-m), three-masted vessel with 34 cannons. Designed for a 150-man crew, it had 23 pairs of oars so the ship could be rowed into position during battle. With sails unfurled, the *Adventure Galley* could make 14 knots, or approximately 16 miles per hour (26 km/h).

Kidd's next job was to find a crew. He expertly handpicked a crew of 70, all experienced sailors and most with families residing in England. His hope was to avoid a repeat of the mutiny he'd had with the pirate crew aboard the *Blessed William* so many years before. His plan was to recruit an additional 80 men in New York.

The sailors signed on knowing that this was a "no purchase-no pay" job. In other words, they would only be paid with shares of looted vessels. Before shares were split, 10 percent of the booty was to be given to the king. Of the remaining treasure, 60 percent would go to the four royal backers, Kidd and Livingstone split 15 percent, and the crew split the remaining 25 percent. With a crew of 150 men, the privateers would need to raid some very treasure-filled ships to make it a profitable venture. Kidd reassured his crew that this would indeed happen.

In February 1696, it seemed that Captain Kidd had everything going for him: royal backing, a strong ship, and a worthy crew. However, Kidd's lucky streak ended with an embarrassing mistake that would cost him dearly.

Facing Page: Eyes for Prize by Don Maitz. *Right:* A ship similar to Kidd's *Adventure Galley.* Artwork by Captain Jeremy Roch.

Costly Disrespect

Captain William Kidd and his crew set sail aboard *Adventure Galley* on February 27, 1696. The ship launched at Deptford, near London, and they began their journey down the River Thames to the sea. On March 1, 1696, as the vessel sailed down the Thames, Kidd made a crucial mistake.

It was English custom to show respect for any Royal Navy vessel by firing a salute. When the *Adventure Galley* passed a Royal Naval ship, it passed without saluting. A shot was fired at the *Adventure Galley* as a reminder. Instead of firing a return salute, several of Kidd's crewmen, who were on the yardarm working the sails, dropped their pants and slapped their backsides—a kind of 17th-century version of "mooning."

An English man-of-war, the HMS *Duchess*, soon stopped the *Adventure Galley*. As punishment, a large number of Kidd's carefully picked crewmen were pressed into service for the Royal Navy. No amount of talk could prevent Captain Kidd from losing his experienced crew.

Kidd found a few replacements, but they were mostly criminals and pirates. The captain had no choice but to sail to New York with exactly the type of crew he did not want.

Below: Men being pressed into service by members of the British navy. Captain William Kidd failed to fire a salute to a Royal Navy ship. To Kidd's great dismay, the commander of the HMS *Duchess* took a large number of Kidd's crewmen into service for the Royal Navy.

Out of Time

Captain Kidd returned to New York in late summer 1696. He needed to recruit men immediately. However, he soon discovered that sailors did not want to sign on to his ship with the shares they were offered.

Kidd was in trouble. He had agreed to complete his mission within a year. If he did not return with the promised booty by March 25, 1697, he would owe his backers a great deal of money. Losing his crew at the start had cost him dearly.

In desperation, Kidd signed on many villainous sailors, agreeing to pay them 60 percent of the profits—the amount Kidd had agreed to give his backers. Governor Fletcher of New York, who would soon be replaced by one of Kidd's backers, Richard Coote, viewed Kidd's efforts with a suspicious eye.

Right: A map showing Kidd's piracy range in light blue.

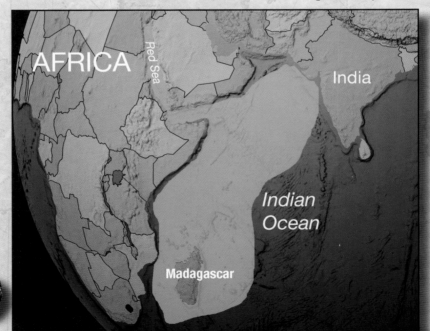

AFRICA

Red Sea

India

Indian Ocean

Madagascar

As though seeing the future, Governor Fletcher wrote to the Board of Trade: "Many flocked to him from all parts, men desperate of fortunes and necessities, in expectation of getting vast treasure. It is generally believed here that if he misses the design named in his commission, he will not be able to govern such a villainous herd."

Kidd had few choices; he had a job to do. After saying goodbye to his wife and daughters, he finally set sail in September 1696 with a crew of 152 men. He was under tremendous pressure to take valuable treasures, but his troubles were just beginning.

Above: Captain William Kidd and crew bury treasure on a remote island. Some believe that his treasure still lies hidden, waiting to be found. Illustration by Howard Pyle.

Privateer or Pirate?

In the fall of 1696, Captain William Kidd sailed to Africa. He intended to cruise around the southernmost point of the continent, the Cape of Good Hope, and then head up to the Indian Ocean. Once there, he fully expected to find both merchant and pirate ships to raid.

The long trip across the Atlantic Ocean was a difficult one. As they neared Cape Town, South Africa, Kidd encountered several Royal Navy ships. Since he held a Royal Commission, Kidd approached one ship, demanding badly needed new sails. The ship's commander, Commodore Thomas Warren, refused.

In his frustration, Kidd vowed to stop the next ship he saw and take what he needed. Warren threatened to seize 30 members of Kidd's crew to serve in the Royal Navy. Kidd could not afford to lose any of his men. That night, Kidd ordered rowers to the oars, slinking silently away.

As 1697 dawned, Kidd headed for Madagascar, an island in the Indian Ocean known as a pirate haven. During the next few months, Kidd sailed up the eastern coast of Africa, heading towards the Red Sea. However, he found no ships to raid. Worse, he lost 50 men to cholera, the dreaded intestinal disease. Plus, the *Adventure Galley* had to be careened and repaired when the hull sprang leaks. The crew became unruly. None of them wanted to go home with nothing to show for a year of their time.

Captain Kidd's deadline to bring treasure to the investors in England came and went. Kidd stayed in the area, no doubt hoping for success.

Kidd attacked several small ships throughout the year, some of which were clearly manned by English allies. Perhaps his need to return money to his financial backers influenced him. Perhaps it was his fear of mutiny. Or maybe he truly believed that these ships were legitimate prizes, falsely sailing under an English flag. Whatever the case, rumors began to flow of the privateer who had turned pirate.

Above: Captain Kidd by Don Maitz.

Kidd Turns Killer

In October 1697, the *Adventure Galley* came across a
Dutch ship, a great prize heavily loaded with trade goods.
Kidd refused to attack the ship, since the Dutch were
allies of the English. A great grumbling arose from the
crew, but Kidd made it clear that if the men left in the
longboats to attack that ship, they would not be returning
to the *Adventure Galley*.

It was an angry crew who continued sailing with Kidd. A
few days after the incident, William Moore, Kidd's gunner,
could hold his tongue no longer. He said to Kidd, "You have
brought us to ruin. We are desolate. I could have put you in
the way of taking that ship and be none the worse for it!"

Kidd replied, "I have not done an ill thing to ruin you.
You are a dog to give me those words." The furious captain
picked up a bucket with iron hoops. He struck Moore's head,
fracturing the gunner's skull. Moore lived one day, and then
died. Kidd was now a murderer.

If the short-tempered captain was regretful of his
mistake, he did not show it. He simply claimed that his
influential friends would see to it that nothing happened
to him because of the incident. But Kidd would be proven
quite wrong.

Facing Page:
Captain Kidd
attacks his gunner.
The unfortunate
crewman died the
next day.

The Quedah Merchant

Kidd and his crew managed to take a few more ships, but in January of 1698, a true prize presented itself. The *Quedah Merchant* was a 400-ton merchant ship flying French flags. An English captain, John Wright, sailed the ship, but he produced a French pass. Kidd believed the ship to be French, and thus according to his commission, he could legally raid it.

However, a large part of the silk, calico, sugar, opium, and iron cargo was owned by a high-ranking official in the Mogul of India's court. After raiding the ship, Kidd sold the cargo, gaining about 7,000 pound sterling, a tidy sum of money.

Finally successful, Kidd went back out to sea. He landed at Madagascar in April 1698, making port in Sainte Marie Harbor. It was there that Kidd came face-to-face with one of the mutineers who had stolen his ship, the *Blessed William*, some 10 years before.

Robert Culliford was a known

Above: A map showing the island of Madagascar, just off the southeast coast of Africa.

pirate. Captain Kidd was commissioned to capture pirates, plus he surely wanted some revenge on this mutinous raider. Surprisingly, instead of capturing Culliford, Kidd joined the pirate for a drink, making no attempt to arrest the scoundrel. Culliford repaid Kidd by departing with most of his crew in June 1698.

Although he had taken quite a prize, Kidd's fortunes began to decline. His ship, the *Adventure Galley*, had rotted. Kidd finally abandoned the vessel, setting it on fire. The *Quedah Merchant* was renamed the *Adventure Prize*. But instead of a prize, the ship would soon become a curse for the unlucky captain.

Kidd's Arrest

Captain Kidd's capture of the *Quedah Merchant*, his one great prize, ended up costing him greatly. Much of the ship's cargo was owned by officials in India. They quickly informed their emperor of their great losses.

Kidd's attack and theft infuriated India's Great Mogul. The leader threatened to end India's association with the British East India Company. This would have been disastrous, not only for the East India Company, but for England as well. The company had a monopoly on trade with India, and this brought in huge amounts of income.

Under pressure, the East India Company paid the owners for the *Quedah Merchant*'s cargo, and sent bribes to Indian officials. The company also agreed to patrol the seas in an attempt to stop future pirate attacks.

Captain Kidd, commissioned to stop pirates, had become one instead. British officials ordered the captain's arrest. In 1698, when a general pardon was issued for all pirates who wished to end their illegal careers, it was specifically noted that this pardon did *not* include William Kidd. A manhunt began for the man who only a few years earlier had been so trusted by some of England's top leaders.

Kidd discovered that he was a wanted man in 1699. Arriving in the Caribbean, he was refused protection by the Danish governor of Saint Thomas. He knew he was in trouble, and so sailed towards home, stopping in New Jersey and at Gardiners Island, New York. It was during these stops that many believe Kidd buried what was left of his treasure. Did he hide it until he could clear his name? Perhaps he honestly believed that he'd done nothing wrong. And yet, he wasn't so trusting as to keep his treasure where it could be easily seized.

Below: A proposal for reducing the pirate population on Madagascar.

Left: Governor Coote, Earl of Bellomont, had William Kidd arrested and sent to London to face charges of piracy.

Kidd ended up in Boston, turning to his friend and financial supporter, Governor Coote, Earl of Bellomont, for help. What Kidd didn't realize was that by his actions, the governor had been placed in a terrible position. Since Governor Coote and the other high officials had backed Kidd, it appeared that they were supporting a pirate. Kidd's backers were charged with improper conduct in office. It was a huge scandal, and the backers needed someone to take responsibility for the misdeeds. Captain William Kidd became the scapegoat. He was arrested in July 1699, and sent to London in April 1700. For Kidd, it was the beginning of the end.

The Trial

Upon arriving in England, Captain Kidd was questioned. He insisted that the taking of the *Quedah Merchant* had been legal because the captain had given a French pass. Kidd blamed any other illegal activities on his pirate crew, who he claimed forced him to commit certain crimes.

Kidd was confined within the cold stone walls of London's Newgate Prison. At first, no one was permitted to see him. But after a few weeks, the rules were relaxed and a few relatives were allowed to visit.

For nearly a year, Newgate remained Kidd's nightmarish home. He finally appeared in court at the House of Commons on March 27, 1701. Questions were shouted at Kidd, but he constantly defended himself, claiming that he was not a pirate.

Kidd's actual trial began on May 8, 1701. The first charge against him was a surprise. For nearly two years he thought he'd be charged with piracy. Instead, the first charge against him was for murder.

Two witnesses, including the ship's surgeon, stated that Kidd had killed gunner William Moore. While Kidd maintained that Moore was a mutineer, the jury found Kidd guilty of murder. Next, Kidd faced the charges of piracy.

Below: One of the "missing" French passes. In the early 1900s, American treasure hunter Ralph Paine found the passes misfiled in a records office in London, England.

The trial was short. Kidd did not have the French passes from the *Quedah Merchant* and the other ship he was accused of wrongfully raiding. He had given the passes to Governor Coote, who by this time had died. The missing passes, which were discovered more than 200 years later in a records office in London, may have made a difference.

Above: Captain Kidd is accused of murder and piracy.

But Kidd had threatened the positions of many high-ranking officials, and they needed him to take responsibility. It would not be surprising if someone in high office had arranged for the passes to "go missing."

    On the following day, William Kidd was found guilty of all charges and sentenced to hang. Kidd's answer was simply, "My Lord, it is a very hard sentence. For my part, I am the innocentest Person of them all…"

Above: Captain Kidd's handwritten note to the King of England. Kidd was ignored.

Treasure and Death

William Kidd's execution was scheduled for Friday, May 23, 1701. Kidd was sentenced to hang with several other guilty souls at Execution Dock at Wapping, London.

Desperate to save himself, Kidd sent a letter to Speaker of the House of Commons Robert Harley. In the letter, Kidd offered to take appointed representatives to a secret place "that in my late proceedings in the Indies I have lodged goods and treasure to the value of one hundred thousand pounds." But the British government refused to spare Kidd's life.

On the day of the hanging, Kidd was so drunk he could barely stand. Loaded into an open cart, the captain was rolled through the streets of London. A massive crowd of 200,000 gathered to scream and taunt. Some came in hope that he would reveal the location of his hidden treasure.

The gallows was on the mudflats of the River Thames, not far from where Kidd's ship, the *Adventure Galley,* had been built and launched. It had been a mere five years since the captain began his privateering adventure, and now he stood in a drunken stupor with a rope around his neck, still maintaining his innocence.

The captain had no dignity, even in death. As the cart was drawn away from the scaffold, the rope around Kidd's neck broke. The unlucky captain dropped into the slimy mud.

Soldiers hurried down to grab the drunken, filth-covered Kidd. Once again he was marched up to the gallows, and a new rope placed around his neck. This time, Captain Kidd danced the hempen jig, strangling to death.

As was the custom with convicted pirates, Kidd's body was left to hang while three tides washed over it. Then, the once-honorable captain's body was covered in tar and hung in a gibbet—an open metal cage—and left dangling.

For years Kidd's body hung in a gory display at the shoreline so that all would know the awful fate that awaited pirates. Nobody wanted to "dry like Kidd." Birds pecked the flesh completely from the captain's body. What was left finally rotted away.

Although his gruesome fate made William Kidd famous, he was far from the most successful pirate. In fact, some historians question whether he could be categorized as a pirate at all. Yet, the name of Captain William Kidd has stayed at the forefront of maritime history for over 300 years. The simple reason is treasure.

Captain Kidd did, in fact, bury his treasure. The stash that he buried on Gardiners Island, New York, was eventually found and dug up by Governor Coote. But did Kidd have more?

Over the course of time, treasure maps have been discovered in furniture believed to be owned by Kidd. While still in jail, Kidd hinted that he had more gold, silver, and jewels stashed away. Was he lying to save his life? Some people think he was telling the truth. The hunt for Captain Kidd's treasure continues to this day.

Above: Captain Kidd's body hung for years as a warning to other pirates.

Glossary

Booty
Money, jewels, and other valuables seized off a ship by raiding pirates.

Bribe
An offer of money or other valuables made in order to sway someone's actions. Often made to government officials to avoid arrest.

Careen
To bring a ship to shore and heave it down onto its side in order to clean or repair the hull.

Caribbean
The islands and area of the Caribbean Sea, roughly the area between Florida and South and Central America.

Cholera
A severe intestinal disease transmitted by contaminated water or food. The extreme diarrhea and vomiting associated with cholera can cause rapid dehydration and result in death.

Dance the Hempen Jig
A crude saying about someone who was executed by hanging. It refers to the spontaneous convulsions of the body that happen during a hanging. The rope used is made from the hemp plant.

Gibbet
An iron cage or structure of chains, hung from a gallows, in which the corpse of an executed criminal was held upright and put on public display to deter others from criminal behavior.

Letter of Marque

Official government document granting a ship's captain permission to use his personal armed vessel for capturing and raiding ships of another country. Used by governments to expand their naval forces at a time of war.

Pirates

Rugged outlaw seamen who capture and raid ships at sea to seize their cargo and other valuables.

Privateer

A ship, or its captain and crew, operating under a letter of marque. A country issued letters of marque to permit the raiding of ships from specified countries that it had engaged in war. The captain and crew were paid out of any booty they took from the ships they attacked. Privateers were also known as "gentlemen pirates."

Scapegoat

A person who bears the blame for others, or who suffers in their place. The term comes from the biblical story in which a goat, symbolically bearing the sins of a people, is sent into the wilderness.

Socialite

A person who is well known among the wealthy and fashionable people in a community.

Yardarm

On a ship, a long, horizontal pole made of wood and tapered toward the ends, used to support and spread a square sail.

Above: People search for Captain Kidd's treasure.

Index